WINTER SPORTS

CURLING

Claire Throp

Raintree
Chicago, Illinois

Edited by Adam Miller, Nancy Dickmann,
    and John-Paul Wilkins
Designed by Richard Parker and Ken Vail Graphic
    Design
Picture research by Elizabeth Alexander
Originated by Capstone Global Library Ltd
Production by Vicki Fitzgerald
Printed and bound in China by Leo Paper
    Products Ltd

17 16 15 14 13
10 9 8 7 6 5 4 3 2 1

**Library of Congress Cataloging-in-Publication
Data**
Throp, Claire.
    Curling / Claire Throp.—1st ed.
        p. cm.—(Winter sports)
    Includes bibliographical references and index.
    ISBN 978-1-4109-5449-7 (hb)—ISBN 978-1-4109-
5455-8 (pb)
    1. Curling—Juvenile literature. I. Title.

GV845.T47 2013
796.964—dc23   2012042734

Acknowledgments
We would like to thank the following for
permission to reproduce photographs: Alamy
pp. 6 (© Mary Evans Picture Library), 15 (© Andrew
Walmsley), 16 (© Tom Wallace/Minneapolis
Star Tribune/ZUMAPRESS. Com), 17, 18, 30 (©
epa european pressphoto agency b.v.), 24 (©
Andres Rodriguez), 27 (© PCN Photography),
31 (© Hipix), 32 (© George S de Blonsky), 38 (©
All Canada Photos), 39 (© IDEAL STOCK), 40 (©
photomadnz), 41 (© CanStock Images); Corbis pp.
4 (© Don Feria/isiphotos.com), 5 (© Barry Lewis/
In Pictures), 7 (© Hulton-Deutsch Collection),
13 bottom (© Jean-Christophe Bott/epa); Getty
Images pp. 10 (Bryn Lennon), 11 (Claus Andersen),
12 (Robyn Beck/AFP), 19 (Fabrice Coffrini/AFP),
20, 37 (Cameron Spencer), 23, 28, 34 (John
MACDOUGALL/AFP), 25 (Claus Fisker/AFP), 29
(Saeed Khan/AFP), 35 (Clive Rose), 36 (Toshifumi
Kitamura/AFP); iStockphoto p. 9 (© The Power
of Forever Photography); Press Association
Images pp. 8 (Robert F. Bukaty/AP), 22 (PA Wire/
PA Archive), 26 (Robert Bukaty/AP); Reuters p. 33
(Russell Cheyne); Shutterstock pp. imprint page
(© Corepics VOF), 9 inset (© Carolina K. Smith,
M.D.), 13 top (© Anton Balazh), 14 (© Bork), 21,
44-45 (© Jerry Zitterman), 42-43 (© Pashin
Georgiy), 47 (© Gemenacom).

Design features reproduced with permission of
Shutterstock (© A'lya, © Allgusak, © Bork, © Eky
Studio, © LehaKoK, © Lonely, © Max Sudakov, ©
Myrtilleshop, © Nicemonkey, © Nik Merkulov, ©
Number One, © secondcorner, © Tanchic, © Vadim
Georgiev).

Cover photo of Northern Ontario skip Brad
Jacobs throwing a rock in a game against Team
Manitoba in the Tim Hortons Brier Canadian
Men's Curling Championship on March 7, 2011,
at the John Labatt Center in London, Canada,
reproduced with permission of Getty Images
(Claus Andersen).

Every effort has been made to contact copyright
holders of material reproduced in this book.
Any omissions will be rectified in subsequent
printings if notice is given to the publisher.

All the Internet addresses (URLs) given in this
book were valid at the time of going to press.
However, due to the dynamic nature of the
Internet, some addresses may have changed, or
sites may have changed or ceased to exist since
publication. While the author and publisher
regret any inconvenience this may cause readers,
no responsibility for any such changes can be
accepted by either the author or the publisher.

CONTENTS

Some words are shown in bold, **like this**. You can find out what they mean by looking in the glossary.

CURLING: A FASCINATING SPORT

It is Canada versus Norway in the men's curling final at the 2002 Winter Olympics. Canada is the clear favorite to win. However, at the final **end**, the teams are tied. Canada still has the last stone advantage and is likely to win. Then, Norway plays an almost perfect end, forcing a mistake from the Canadians. Norway wins the gold medal.

Curling is known as...

Curling is similar to playing shuffleboard on ice. The aim is to slide stones toward the center of a target, and the stones that end up closest to the center win points. The name "curling" comes from the way that the stone curls across the ice.

Curling is sometimes known as "chess on ice." This is because **strategy** plays such an important role in the game. Figuring out the path and placement of a stone takes a lot of planning. It is also known as the "roaring game" because of the noise the stone makes as it moves across the ice.

Concentration is important when a player is about to deliver a stone.

Which are the top teams?

Curling is played in 49 countries, including the United States, Canada, the United Kingdom, Norway, Sweden, and China. The game is particularly popular in Canada, which dominates the men's game. Great Britain and Norway are also top men's teams. Sweden and Canada are the top women's teams.

"Curling is getting a little bit more popular because of the Olympics. We want to be able to promote the sport because it's not very well known."

– Cassie Johnson, U.S. **skip**

Curling is mainly played indoors today, but if it is cold enough, it can still be played outside.

This book will look at some basic rules of curling and how to play. It will also focus on the major championships and some of the best-known players.

A HISTORY OF CURLING

Many believe curling began in Scotland, because the first written mention of curling comes from Scotland, in 1540. Others think that curling was first played in the Low Countries (now the Netherlands, Belgium, and Luxembourg). Artist Pieter Breughel included Dutch peasants playing a game that looks like curling in two of his paintings dated 1565. There was trade between Great Britain and the Low Countries at this time, but it is not certain which country introduced the game to the other.

NO WAY!

The oldest known curling stone—the Stirling Stone—was found in Dunblane, Scotland. "1511" is marked on its side. It's about half the size of a modern curling stone and square rather than round.

Scottish immigrants brought curling to Canada in the 1700s and then to the United States in the early 1800s. The Montreal Curling Club was set up in Canada in 1807, and the first U.S. club appeared near Detroit, Michigan, in 1832.

The Grand Caledonian Curling Club, set up in Scotland in 1838, became the **governing body**. This helped to standardize curling in North America, too.

This woman was a competitor in the first Scottish outdoor tournament of 1959.

Early competitions

Curling was first played at the Olympics in 1924 (see page 27), while the Scotch Cup is considered the first world championship. It was first held in Scotland in 1959 between teams from Scotland and Canada. A Canadian team won. The World Championships soon became an established part of international competition, and Olympic participation came in 1998. Other tournaments have been added over the years, including junior and wheelchair championships.

THE BASICS

The aim of curling is to get your stones closer to the **tee** than the other team in order to win points. The team with the most points wins. The area on which a curling game is played is called the **curling sheet**.

The ice

While skaters need wet ice, so that their skates can move smoothly over it, curlers need to have a dry surface with a "pebble" of water droplets on top. Before a game, an ice technician uses a **pebbling** machine that sprays a fine mist of hot water over the flat ice surface. Soon, there is a layer of tiny bumps on the surface of the ice. These mean that the running edge on the bottom of each stone has minimal contact with the flat ice, allowing it to glide smoothly. As a game goes on and the pebble wears down, stones start to travel shorter distances and curl more.

An ice technician prepares the ice for play with a pebbling machine.

Curling sheet layout

The **sheet** is 150 feet (46 meters) long, with a maximum width of 16.5 feet (5 meters). There is a target at either end called the **house**. It consists of three rings of different colors. The center of the house is known as the tee or **button** and is where the tee line and center line meet.

center line

hog line

free guard zone

house

tee line

back line

tee/button

hack

Hacks

Hacks are rubber foot holds that are placed 6 feet (1.8 meters) behind the back lines. Players use one of the hacks to push against when delivering a stone.

This diagram shows one half of a curling sheet. When an end is complete, the next end starts from the opposite end of the sheet.

The team

A curling team is known as a **rink**. It is made up of four players: lead, second, third, and the skip. The lead delivers the first and second stones, the second delivers the third and fourth stones, and third (or vice-skip) delivers the fifth and sixth stones. The last two stones are delivered by the skip, or captain, of the team. Each player alternates with his or her equivalent on the opposing team. One of the most important parts of curling is how well the team works together. This helps the team to run smoothly and often brings success.

CASSIE JOHNSON

Born: October 30, 1981, in Bemidji, Minnesota
Nationality: American
Known for: Silver medal winner at the 2005 World Championships; skip of the U.S. team at the 2006 Winter Olympics
Interesting fact: Cassie's sister, Jamie, also plays on the U.S. curling team

Against the clock

A game is made up of 8 or 10 ends played against the clock. Each team has 73 minutes to complete all 10 ends (59 minutes to complete 8 ends), and there is a five-minute break after five ends. If a team goes over this time limit, it loses the game.

house

Glossary of terms

button   center of the house and also known as the tee; stones closest to the button win the points

curling sheet   place where the game is played

end   period of time during which each player throws two stones. Games have either 8 or 10 ends.

hog line   line that goes across the width of the curling sheet. Players must release the stone before they reach this line.

house   area within the circles at each end of the curling sheet

rink   team or the name of the place where curling is played (ice rink)

skip   captain of the team

tee line   line that goes across the width of the curling sheet, passing through the center of the tee and parallel to the hog line

The free guard rule

The **free guard zone** is the area between the **hog line** and tee line, but not including the house. The free guard rule states that any stones in the free guard zone cannot be knocked out of play by an opponent's stone until the first two stones from each side have been delivered. If they are knocked out, then they are replaced, and the stone that hit them is taken out of play.

Measuring devices, like this one, measure the distance from the nearest part of the stone to the tee.

Scoring

Each stone that is within the house and closer to the button than the opposition's stones wins a point. Only one team can score in each end. If the score is even after 10 ends, an extra end is played. Whichever team scores first wins. Sometimes it can be difficult to tell which team's stone is the closest to the button when an end finishes, so a measuring device is used.

NO WAY!

Russ Howard, a Canadian skip, caused a change in rules because he was losing his voice during the 1989 **Brier** while yelling instructions. He started using a two-way radio. The match officials asked him not to use the radio in the next match. However, there was nothing in the rules to say radios were not allowed, so Howard used it again in the following match. Officials were forced to change the rules before the next round to state that no radios would be allowed. It was the first time that a new rule had been introduced in the middle of a competition.

The skip is the person who leads the team and decides strategy.

EQUIPMENT

Curling stones are made from a strong rock called granite. They each weigh about 42 pounds (19 kilograms) and have a plastic handle on top. A ring, called the running edge, on the bottom of the stone is the only part of the stone to touch the ice. Apart from the striking band (a band of granite in the middle of the stone) and the running edge, the rest of the stone is highly polished. When the striking band hits another stone, it forces it to move in the opposite direction—which is good for getting rid of an opponent's stone.

handle

striking band

Curling stones used in the Olympics come from the Scottish island of Ailsa Craig and are sometimes known as Ailsas. The island is now a reserve for the Royal Society for the Protection of Birds (RSPB), and although blasting is forbidden, loose rocks are still taken to make curling stones. Other stones are made from granite quarried in Trefor, Wales.

The unique properties of Ailsa Craig granite make it perfect for curling stones.

Brushes

A brush or broom is an essential piece of equipment for any curler. Everyone on the team except the skip uses a brush to **sweep**. They all use the brush for balance when delivering a stone. Originally, a hoghair or horsehair brush was used, but most curlers now use brushes with **synthetic** pads.

No Way!

Using a broom to sweep the ice in front of a stone comes from the sport originally being played on a frozen lake, and so players had to sweep away the snow before they could deliver a shot. Thankfully, the players don't have to deal with snow anymore!

15

Clothing

Since the game of curling is played on ice, warm clothing is usually necessary! The clothes should be comfortable to wear. There are pants designed specifically for curling. They need to be stretchy to allow for a big range of movement, particularly when delivering a stone. They look very similar to tracksuit bottoms. Gloves are also worn and are usually made of calfskin or deerskin. They need to fit well, or they may cause blisters from all the sweeping. Some players wear mittens, but most find that gloves are better for gripping the brush.

Slider shoes have smooth pads so they can glide across the ice.

Shoes

The most important thing to get is the right type of shoes. When delivering a stone, one foot needs to be able to slide along the ice. The bottom of the shoe needs to be covered in a low-friction material, such as Teflon. This shoe needs to be protected when not on the ice, since it is easily damaged. Some players use a slider that slips onto the bottom of the shoe and can be removed easily when they step off the ice. The other shoe needs to be able to grip the ice, so it usually has a rubber sole that prevents slipping.

THOMAS ULSRUD

Born: October 21, 1971, in
Oslo, Norway

Nationality: Norwegian

Started curling: 1981

Known for: Being skip for
Norway; winner of silver medal at
2010 Winter Olympics

Interesting fact: Became well
known at the 2010 Winter
Olympics for wearing the
"loudest" pants you have
ever seen!

HOW TO PLAY

To deliver a stone, a player holds it close to his or her toes, pushes off from the hack, slides forward, and then releases the stone. At this point, a player can use the handle to make the stone curl clockwise (known as an in-turn) or counterclockwise (known as an out-turn). The stone must be released before it crosses the hog line. It must then cross the far hog line in order to be in play.

The three main shots are:

- The draw: This gets a stone into the house.
- The **guard**: This places a stone at the front of the house to protect the stone nearest the tee (the one that will score a point) from the opposition's stones.
- The hit: This removes one or more of your opponent's stones from play.

When delivering a stone, a player has to be careful not to put too much force into the release, or the stone may not go in the required direction.

Sweeping

Sweeping the ice in front of the stone helps to control how far the stone travels and also the direction it moves in. Sweeping melts the ice slightly, allowing the stone to travel farther and straighter. All team members can sweep between the tee lines, but beyond the tee line, only one player is allowed to sweep.

NO WAY!

Good, experienced players can help the stone to move an additional 5 to 6 feet (1.5–1.8 meters) by sweeping. That is about the height of an adult.

Strategy

Strategy—deciding what shot to play—is very important in the game of curling. At the start of a match, teams flip a coin to see who gets last stone advantage. This is when a team gets to deliver the final stone of an end, which is known as the hammer. Whichever team scores in an end then takes the first stone in the next end. Strategy for an end is usually based on whether or not the team has last stone advantage. Earlier stones can set up what hopefully can be finished off with the final delivery—although it depends on the other team, of course!

The skip usually stands behind the tee so that he or she can determine what the best path for the next stone will be. When the skip is delivering the stone, the vice-skip takes this role. While the skip makes the final decision about the placement of a stone, team discussions occur before each end and often before each shot.

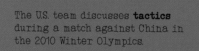

The U.S. team discusses **tactics** during a match against China in the 2010 Winter Olympics.

Adapting

The position of stones in the house may change after every stone is delivered, so plans have to be adapted all the time to suit the situation. This involves quick thinking and decision making. For example, one of the things a skip might need to consider is: What if the next shot is missed? What could be the consequences? The ice also has an effect on how stones move, so that can also affect strategy. All kinds of tactics that are not always obvious to the spectators may come into play.

Each team has a set of stones of the same color. In major championships, the colors used are usually red and yellow.

THE SPIRIT OF CURLING

Curling has a reputation of sportsmanship, perhaps more so than any other sport. There is a handshake before and after a game, and players wish each other "Good curling." If any rules are broken, curlers usually admit to it. For example, if a player touches one of the opposition's stones as it is in motion (known as burning the stone), he or she is expected to declare this to the officials. Respect for fellow curlers is a very important part of the game.

"Curlers never knowingly break a rule of the game, nor disrespect any of its traditions...the spirit of curling demands good sportsmanship, kindly feeling, and honorable conduct."

– Part of the World Curling Federation rules of curling document

Sportsmanship awards

Both men and women have the opportunity to win a sportsmanship award at the World Championships. For the men, the award is called the Collie Campbell Award. The women's version is known as the Frances Brodie Award. These awards are voted for by the players in the tournament. There are also awards made in the junior and wheelchair curling championships.

> "Curlers do not need an umpire or a referee or rules. They govern themselves as gentlemen."
>
> – Collie Campbell, former president of the International Curling Federation

RUSS HOWARD

Born: February 19, 1956, Ontario, Canada

Nationality: Canadian

Job: When he isn't curling, Russ works in real estate, does some commentating, and also coaches in Switzerland

Known for: 2006 Winter Olympic gold medal winner and developer of the Moncton rule (now called the free guard zone rule, one of the main rules now used in international competition)

Interesting fact: Russ is the oldest Canadian ever to win an Olympic gold medal

FITNESS AND MENTAL STRENGTH

Perhaps the most important way for players to improve their skills is to practice, but there are other things that can have an effect on how well they play.

If players want to be successful at curling, they have to train hard. Gym work is just part of the training they do every day.

Fitness

Fitness was not always seen as essential to the sport of curling—in fact, there was a view that it was only played by old, overweight people! However, these days, most professional curlers are very fit. Pre-season training is now standard. Curling matches last about two hours, and in major tournaments, more than one game can be played in a day. This means that **stamina**—being able to keep playing at a high level for a long time—is also important.

It's all in the mind

Players often talk about mental preparation being important for winning matches, but what does this mean? Thinking positively, being confident, staying relaxed, being motivated, and wanting to win are some of the things that top players do to stay at the top. Trying to get inside the mind of your opponents can help, too.

"A team that is fit and has done its mental preparations probably has an edge on other teams."

— Shannon Kleibrink, skip for Canada at the 2006 Winter Olympics

"It used to be a hobby. It's nice to be able to say that we're athletes now. We train just as hard as other sports do. We live, sleep, eat, and breathe curling."

— Jackie Lockhart, British curling team member, 2009

CHAMPIONSHIPS AND TOURNAMENTS

There are a number of different international competitions for curling as well as national tournaments and local leagues and events.

Sweden celebrates after beating Canada in the 2010 Winter Olympics.

The Winter Olympics

The Winter Olympics come around once every four years and represent the main tournament for most players. There are two separate tournaments—one for women and one for men. In major championships like the Olympics, teams can have a fifth player known as an alternate. The players can be swapped from game to game, but not within a game.

Teams can get points for Olympic qualification from World Championships in the two years running up to the Olympic year. The seven top teams qualify for the Olympics and are joined by the host team. An additional two teams will qualify for the Olympics by doing well at an Olympic Qualification Event held the year before the Olympics.

USA 🇺🇸 42-52

GER

Olympic sport

Curling has been an official Olympic sport since 1998, but its first appearance (for men only) came in the Winter Games at Chamonix, France, in 1924. Curling was a **demonstration sport** at the 1924 games, which meant the winners were not officially recognized. However, over 80 years later, in 2006, the International Olympic Committee made curling an official event, and the medals awarded in 1924 were given official status. The gold medal winner was Great Britain.

NAIL-BITING MOMENT!

In the 2010 Winter Olympics, the U.S. team lost three matches in a row on the very last shot of the game. Unlucky!

The format of Olympic curling

At the Olympics, 10 teams play a "**round robin**" format, meaning each team plays every other team once. The top four teams go into the quarterfinals. The winner of a game between the first- and second-place teams goes straight into the final, while the loser goes to the semifinal. They are joined by the winner of the match between the third- and fourth-place teams. The winner of the semifinal meets the team that went through automatically to the final.

RHONA MARTIN

Born: October 12, 1966, in Irvine, Scotland

Nationality: Scottish

Job: Works as an elite coach with the Scottish Institute of Sport and was a TV commentator during the 2010 Winter Olympics

Known for: Skip of Great Britain team that won the 2002 Winter Olympics, Great Britain's first Winter Olympics gold medal in 18 years

Interesting fact: Rhona carried the Olympic torch through Glasgow, Scotland, in June 2012

Olympic gold medal winners

Women
1998 Canada
2002 Great Britain
2006 Sweden
2010 Sweden

Men
1924 Great Britain
1998 Switzerland
2002 Norway
2006 Canada
2010 Canada

Paralympics

Wheelchair curling made its first appearance at the 2006 **Paralympic** Winter Games in Turin, Italy. Teams have four people and must include men and women. No sweeping is allowed in wheelchair curling. Delivery of the stones can be done by using an extender cue, a type of stick. In 2010, 10 teams competed in Vancouver, Canada. Canada won the gold medal in 2006 and 2010.

Canada's men celebrate after receiving their gold medals at the 2010 Winter Olympics in Vancouver, Canada.

The World Championships

The top 12 curling nations come together once a year to compete in the World Curling Championships. The men's tournament was first played in 1959 and was well established by the time the women's event started in 1979. Few spectators went to the women's event, so from 1989 to 2004, the two tournaments were held together. Since 2005, the men's and women's events have been held separately. This is because it was felt that the women's game now had a decent following, and it also allows major curling events to be taken to more places.

NO WAY!

In 1968, Air Canada **sponsored** the world championship and called it the Air Canada Silver Broom. What was the prize given to the winners? A silver broom!

The 2012 World Men's Curling Championships took place in Switzerland. In this match, Scotland plays against Canada.

The format

The format of the World Championships is the same as the Olympics—round robin followed by the playoffs—but with two extra teams. More than 30 countries try to get a place at the World Championships, so teams have to play regional championships to determine who gets the available places. Europe gets eight places, North America gets two places, and the Pacific region (including Australia, China, and Japan) gets two places.

NAIL-BITING MOMENT!

The Women's World Championship final of 2006 was one of the closest matches of all time. The United States had only 50 seconds left on the clock to make the last delivery. The shot had to be rushed and left Sweden with a good chance to win. The winner of the gold medal was…Sweden!

Curling is so popular in Canada that there are even postage stamps celebrating it!

The World Wheelchair Curling Championships

Switzerland and Sweden were the first countries to try wheelchair curling in 2000. The first World Wheelchair Curling Championship took place in Switzerland in 2002. The home nation won. The championship now takes place every year, except the year when the Paralympic Winter Games happen.

Tom Killin releases a stone during a match between Great Britain and the United States at the 2006 Winter Paralympic Games in Turin, Italy.

Other tournaments

An annual Junior World Championship has been played since 1975 for men and since 1988 for women. There are 10 teams, and players must be under the age of 21. More recently, a Senior World Championship has been set up for the over-50s, in addition to a Mixed Doubles World Championship in which one man and one woman plays on each team. The European Championship is played once a year among 37 curling nations. Sweden is dominant in the women's game, while Scotland has won the most men's championships.

National championships

The United States Men's Curling Championship and the United States Women's Curling Championship are each held once a year. These events help decide who might move on to the World Championship level.

A Japan's women's team competes at the World Junior Curling Championships in Scotland in 2011.

WATCHING CURLING

Curling has become more and more popular since its entrance into the Olympic Games. Watching curling is something many people now do, either by going to matches or watching on television.

Curling live

Going to see matches locally and at major championships is a pastime enjoyed by millions of people. The total number of spectators at Canadian men's tournaments regularly hits 200,000. There is nothing like going to a live sporting event and hearing everyone cheering for their team and celebrating success.

Volunteering

Volunteering at a tournament is another way to get involved with the sport. Hundreds of volunteers are needed at big events to help with things like selling programs, serving food and drinks, and security. It is a great way to see what goes on behind the scenes at a tournament.

NAIL-BITING MOMENT!

In the men's final at the 2006 Winter Olympics, Canada was in trouble. One of Finland's stones was on the button and protected by lots of Finnish guard stones. Mark Nichols, the Canadian third, made an amazing shot. His stone hit a guard, which knocked into another guard, which then knocked Finland's stone off the button. Canada was left with three stones closest to the button and took the points. It made for exciting viewing!

ANETTE NORBERG

Born: November 12, 1966, in Härnösand, Sweden
Nationality: Swedish
Lives: Härnösand, Sweden
Known for: Winning two Olympic golds as Swedish skip, as well as three World Championships and seven European Championships
Interesting fact: Anette played in the Olympic demonstration event for curling in 1992

Built for television

An American curling commentator, Don Chevrier, once suggested that curling was "built for television." This is because there is space for cameras at either end of the sheet, and the players wear microphones so that viewers can hear what they talk about during the team meetings between ends. Not only does the team's strategy get discussed, but listening in on all the stress and tension of playing in a major tournament can help to make the game more exciting for the viewer.

There are often several curling sheets in a curling arena. Here, several teams compete alongside each other at the 2010 Winter Olympics in Vancouver, Canada.

NO WAY!

Curling was not a well-known sport in the United States before the 2002 Olympics. In the Olympics of 2002 and 2006, curling was one of the most watched winter sports on television in the United States. In February 2006, about 100 million people visited the United States Curling Association's web site. This was the year the United States won bronze.

Big viewing figures

Curling has become one of the most popular televised Winter Games sports, particularly in North America. In Canada, the finals of the men's and women's National Championships have been watched by over a million people. Millions of people also watch curling events in one of the newer curling nations, China.

Curling can be an exciting game to watch as the tension rises.

NAIL-BITING MOMENT!

In the women's Olympic final in 2010, Canada and Sweden were playing a tense, close match. Canada skip Cheryl Bernard's last stone of the 10th end failed to curl as much as she wanted, and the Swedish skip, Anette Norberg, was able to force an extra end. Bernard's last throw in the 11th end overcurled and left one Swedish stone still in play. The Swedes celebrated—they had beaten Canada 7–6, to win the gold.

CURLING IS FOR EVERYONE

Curling is a game that can be played by anyone, from children to the elderly. Age is not important, because neither speed nor a lot of physical strength is essential. There are lighter stones for children to use. There are no inequalities—curling can be played by men and women on the same team (mixed). Age is not even an issue at the international level. Eve Muirhead was made Great Britain's skip at the age of just 19, while Russ Howard was 50 when he helped Canada win gold in 2006.

As long as you're reasonably fit, your age shouldn't stop you from enjoying curling.

EVE MUIRHEAD

Born: April 22, 1990, in Perth, Scotland

Nationality: Scottish

Lives: Blair Atholl, Perthshire, Scotland

Known for: Four-time world junior women's champion and skip of Great Britain in the 2010 Winter Olympics

Interesting fact: Eve is also excellent at playing the bagpipes, having performed in four World Championships!

Curling for disabled athletes

There are teams for wheelchair curling, people who are visually impaired, and those who are hearing impaired. Wheelchair curling is usually played by mixed teams. There are currently 24 countries taking part in wheelchair curling. Players who take part in wheelchair curling have lower body impairments and usually need wheelchairs for everyday life. Visually impaired curling might sound difficult, if not impossible, but it is a fast-growing version of the game. Hearing impaired curling is also becoming more common, with a World Championship already set up.

Could curling be the game for you?

In the United States, there are about 16,000 people who curl. Canada has 1.2 million curlers! While international competitors train hard and have high levels of fitness, people playing casually at local clubs can decide how much they want to put into the sport. Many clubs have open days, known as open houses, that allow people to try the game for the first time. There are also "Learn to Curl" classes available. Most clubs offer a learn-to-curl clinic (half-day or full day) at the beginning of the season. It is usually a case of "try it for free," so if you decide you don't like curling, you have not wasted money.

Curling is a sport that is usually played indoors on ice rinks. However, sometimes it can take place outside in front of spectacular scenery.

Curling facilities in the United States are not always easy to find, but the United States Curling Association web site will have helpful information (see page 46). Open days for curling allow people to try the game for the first time.

Give it a try!

Curling may not be a particularly well-known sport, but since its inclusion in the 1998 Winter Olympics, more and more people have become interested in the game. The numbers of people playing, watching live, and watching on television have increased all over the world. Curling is a fun and challenging sport to take up. Why not give it a try yourself?

NO WAY!

Even the Simpsons have curled! In one episode of *The Simpsons,* Homer and Marge became part of a mixed doubles team that represents the United States in the Olympics. The episode was shown on television during the 2010 Winter Olympics.

Kids can curl, too! Ask your parents or caregiver to take you to a local club and see how much fun it is to join in.

QUIZ

How much do you know about curling?
Test yourself with these questions.

1. Which member of a team does not usually sweep?

a) vice-skip

b) lead

c) skip

2. Which women's team has won the Olympics twice?

a) Canada

b) Sweden

c) Great Britain

3. How many countries play wheelchair curling?

a) 15

b) 24

c) 45

4. In what year did the United States women's team win a silver medal at the World Championships?

a) 2005

b) 1999

c) 1976

5. What's the maximum width of a curling sheet?

a) 33 feet (10 meters)

b) 16.5 feet (5 meters)

c) 6.5 feet (200 centimeters)

6. What type of material is often used on the bottom of a curling shoe?

a) wood

b) copper

c) Teflon

7. Who helped to develop the free guard zone rule?

a) Homer Simpson

b) Cassie Johnson

c) Russ Howard

8. What is pebbling?

a) spraying the surface of the ice with hot water before a game

b) throwing pebbles onto the ice to try to trip up the opposition

c) a victory dance done by any team that wins a major competition

7–8 correct answers: Clearly, you know your stuff when it comes to curling! Perhaps you could be competing for medals in the future.

4–6 correct answers: Not bad. Try to join a club in your area and get some practice in.

1–3 correct answers: There is so much to learn about curling. Try to watch some on television or on the Internet and see if you can learn more about it. You might find you want to play!

Answers

1. c
2. b
3. b
4. a
5. b
6. c
7. c
8. a

GLOSSARY

Brier annual Canadian men's curling championship

button small circle at the center of the house; also known as the tee. The main object of curling is to get the stones as close to the button as possible.

curling sheet area of ice where the game of curling is played

demonstration sport sport played at the Olympics before it is officially accepted as an Olympic sport. No medals are given out for demonstration sports.

end period of time during which each player throws two stones. Games have either eight or ten ends. An end is similar to an inning in baseball.

free guard zone area at the playing end between the hog line and the tee line, but not including the house

governing body group that ensures everyone plays a sport according to the same rules and standards around the world

guard stone that is placed so that it protects another stone in the house

hack foothold at the end of the ice from which players push off when delivering a stone

hog line line that goes across the width of the curling sheet. Players must release the stone before they reach this line.

house area within the circles at each end of the curling sheet

Paralympic relating to the Paralympics, an international competition for disabled athletes that takes place every four years

pebbling method of preparing the ice for a curling game, in which water is sprayed onto the ice in order to reduce friction between the stone and the ice

rink curling team, or the name of the place where curling is played (ice rink)

round robin competition format in which each team plays every other team once

sheet *see* curling sheet

skip captain of a team who also decides strategy during the game

sponsor to support an organization or sport by giving money or other assistance

stamina ability to keep going for long periods of time without tiring too much, particularly while taking part in sports

strategy planning how to go about something—for example, winning a game of curling

sweep when players move their brushes back and forth in front of a moving stone in order to change its direction or make it go further

synthetic human-made, using chemicals

tactic action or technique used to achieve a desired goal

tee *see* button

volunteer do something you don't have to, usually without expecting to be paid

FIND OUT MORE

Books

Bekkering, Annalise. *Curling* (For the Love of Sports). New York: Weigl, 2007.

Hunter, Nick. *The Winter Olympics*. Chicago: Heinemann Library, 2014.

Johnson, Robin. *Ice Hockey and Curling* (Winter Olympic Sports). New York: Crabtree, 2010.

Weeks, Bob. *Curling, Etcetera: A Whole Bunch of Stuff About the Roaring Game*. Hoboken, N.J.: John Wiley and Sons, 2009.

Web sites

www.olympic.org/curling
The official Olympic web site has a section about curling.

www.usacurl.org/usacurl
Learn more about the curling scene in the United States on the United States Curling Association's web site.

www.uswca.org/content/sport-curling.asp
The United States Women's Curling Association web site is full of information about how women can get involved in the game.

www.worldcurling.org
This is the web site of the World Curling Federation.

Topics to research

- Find out how a sport goes from being a demonstration sport to an official Olympic one.

- Learn about which exercises are best for different aspects of curling.

- Research the history of curling, particularly in your own country.

INDEX